# Michael M. Dediu

------------------------------

# The
# Constitution
of the **World**

---

Moving from many unsustainable
constitutions, to just one
Constitution of the World

---

**DERC Publishing House**

Tewksbury (Boston), Massachusetts, U. S. A.

Published and printed in the
United States of America
On the Great Seal of the United States are included:
E Pluribus Unum (Out of many, one)
Annuit Coeptis (He has approved of the undertakings)
Novus Ordo Seclorum (New order of the ages)

**Library of Congress Control Number: 2020904140**

Dediu, Michael M.

The Constitution of the World
Moving from many unsustainable constitutions, to just one
Constitution of the World

ISBN-13: 978-1-950999-10-1

MSG0314221_cZ8oX8f1oXHU144MhKKW
MSG0315146_34pt498VK9KURgJ2ID1u
MSG0315145_7wKMBI61iVi4Io9dLA90
1-8615371801
1-3YHDBGU
26O3F7K8

# Preface

There are now over 190 unsustainable constitutions, which often bring conflicts, confrontations and wars - the big family of over 7.7 billions of people living on Earth want a brand new, sharp, clear, peaceful, friendly and sustainable Constitution of the World, which will finally eliminate wars, nuclear arms, and many other deadly habits of the past.

With this new lovely Constitution people can start the next 10,000 years of harmony, after the last 10,000 years of conflicts.

In this book we present this very needed Constitution of the World, which will create the conditions for a nonviolent, free and prosperous new country, Peaceful Terra.

Michael M. Dediu, Ph. D.

Tewksbury (Boston), U. S. A., 6 March 2020

USA: 11 July 2009, tall ship at the northwest side of Boston Fish Pier in Boston (1630, population 650,000) Harbor (Port of Boston has 200 ha, draft depth 12 m, 237,000 containers/year; the Boston Harborwalk provides public access to much of the harbor's edge).

# Table of Contents

Italy, Venice: Il Torre dell'Orologio (the Clock Tower) is on the north side of the Piazza San Marco (1499). On the top of the Torre there are two big bronze statues, hinged at the waist, which strike the hours on the bell. One is old and the other young and they are wearing sheepskins. The Winged Lion of Venice is below the bell and holds the book quoting "Pax Tibi Marce Evangelista Meus" (Peace to you Mark my evangelist).

# The Constitution of the World

## Proposition 1. We, the People of the World

We, the People on this Earth, in order to

    1.1 - completely eliminate war and any type of conflicts,

    1.2 - have a peaceful and harmonious world,

    1.3 - have freedom, dignity, good families and respect,

    1.4 - have good health and good education,

    1.5 - have a friendly atmosphere and prosperity,

    1.6 – have the safety and wellbeing of all the people in the world as the highest priority,

    1.7 – use the best peaceful results, experience and knowledge of all current countries,

establish this Constitution of the World.

Italy, Venice: Libreria Sansoviniana (left), Il Campanile (center-left), Palazzo Ducale (right), and a Japanese couple wedding picture.

## Proposition 2. Peaceful Terra

2.1 - All the people of the world will be proud citizens of only one country, called Peaceful Terra, with total area of over 509 M km$^2$, and land area over 148 M km$^2$.

2.2 - All the rules – not more than 2,000, on maximum 1,000 pages - on our Earth will be established by the people and their elected Advisers.

USA, Washington (1790), National Gallery of Art (1937, National Mall)

## Proposition 3. Ten Simple and Friendly Regions

3.1 - For easier administration, Peaceful Terra will be only administratively divided in 10 simple and friendly regions of around 770 M people each, called R0, R1,…, R9, which will be delimited by meridians (or line of longitudes), with the assistance of the United Nations.

3.2 - Each region will have a pair of capitals plus an outside city, for better and more homogenous management (all will change every year; more details are in the annex book "World with One Country & its Ten Friendly Regions - Moving from 195 disagreeing countries, to 1 country with 10 collaborating regions"). For example, the first implementation will be:
R0 between meridians 0 and $15^0$ E, capitals: Bern (Switzerland), Libreville (Gabon), and Oxford (UK).

UK, London: The meridian 0 (Prime meridian, 1851, official 1884, stainless steel strip under the man in red), Flamsteed House (1676, center up).

R1: $15^0$ E - $30^0$ E, Warsaw (Poland), Pretoria (South Africa) and Miami (FL, USA).

R2: $30^0$ E - $45^0$ E, Moscow (Russia), Cairo (Egypt), and Grenoble (France).

R3: $45^0$ E - $75^0$ E, Astana (Kazakhstan), Karachi (Pakistan), and Montpellier (France).

R4: $75^0$ E - $85^0$ E, New Delhi (India), Novosibirsk (Russia), and Magdeburg (Germany).

R5: $85^0$ E - $100^0$ E, Krasnoyarsk (Russia), Urumqi (China), and Avignon (France).

R6: $100^0$ E - $115^0$ E, Jakarta (Indonesia), Beijing (China), and Neuchâtel (Switzerland).

R7: $115^0$ E - $180^0$, Tokyo (Japan), Sydney (Australia), and Malmö (Sweden).

R8: $180^0$ - $70^0$ Washington (USA), Mexico City (Mexico), and Bellinzona (Switzerland).

R9: $70^0$ W – 0 Halifax (Canada), Brasilia (Brazil), and Biel (Switzerland).

France, Paris: The Institut de France (1795, initially in Louvre, moved in 1805 by Napoléon in this baroque building finished in 1684, for Collège des Quatre-Nations) is a revered French cultural society which includes five académies, the most famous being Académie française (1635) and. Académie des sciences (Academy of Sciences), founded in 1666. The Institute, located on Quai de Conti, manages about 1,000 foundations, as well as museums and châteaux. Its Mazarine Library is France's oldest public library.

3.2. Each of the 10 regions will be divided by meridians in 10 sub-regions S00,    , S99, each with about 77 M people.

3.3. Each of the 100 sub-regions will be divided in 10 districts D000, D001,    , D999, each with about 7.7 M people, and each of the districts will have their current small and big cities.

3.4. Having telework, many people will have a northern residence and a southern residence, seasonally moving from one to the other, to avoid extreme cold or heat, and having the same hour.

3.5. All the oceans will belong to some of the regions defined above, therefore will be maintained by those regions, to be free of any piracy or other bad activity – World Police will help when necessary.

Italy, Venice, Piazza San Marco: The west façade of the Palazzo Ducale (Doge's Palace), 1420.

## Proposition 4. No borders

4.1 - In Peaceful Terra there are no borders.

4.2 - There will be just simple administrative delimitations, and all these delimitations between regions, as well as between sub-regions, will be flexible – they will be changed after each census (5 years), for maintaining a balanced number of people in all regions (around 770 M) and sub-regions (around 77 M).

4.3 - In the first implementation presented in Proposition 3, there are many big differences between the populations of different regions, and then between the populations of different sub-regions, but this is just the first implementation, which needs to be quickly put in place, and then, very easily, the delimitations will be moved a few kilometers east or west, to reach a balanced population.

4.4 - Because all the people are in the same country, it is normal to modify a little its regions, for better administration, to make everybody happy.

4.5 - It is well understood that there will be some difficulties in the beginning, like in all beginnings, but with calm, patience, perseverance and hard work, the things will improve fast, and all the people will enjoy a better life.

London, from the Shard (2012, 309 m, observatory at 244 m), looking east to the Tower Bridge (1886-1894, combined bascule and suspension turreted bridge over River Thames (flowing from west (left) to east (right)), between London boroughs Tower Hamlets (north – left up) and Southwark (south – right), length 244 m, height 65 m, longest span 82 m, clearance 8 m (closed), 42 m (open)), City Hall (2002, height 45 m, center right round, for the Greater London Authority: Mayor of London and the London Assembly).

# Proposition 5. The Government of Peaceful Terra

## 5.1. The family of over 7. 7 B people

from Peaceful Terra will have four levels of world management; at the local level, if needed, it could be one or two more levels of local managers (mayors, town managers, county managers – all levels of management must be friendly, helpful, fast, polite, modest and smart):

## 5.2. Level 1 Management: 1,000 L1 friendly managers

1,000 L1 friendly managers for the 1,000 districts, who will supervise and assist the mayors and town managers from their district, for a total of about 7,700,000 people in each district. Each of the 1,000 L1 friendly managers will be located in a central city from their districts – they could be the mayors of those cities, but with new responsibilities for the whole district.

## 5.3. Level 2 Management: 100 L2 friendly managers

100 L2 friendly managers for the 100 sub-regions, who will supervise and assist the 10 L1 managers of the 10 districts of each sub-region, for a total of about 77,000,000 people for each sub-region. These 100 L2 friendly managers will move each month between the two capitals of each of the 100 sub-regions.

In the beginning these capitals will be:

Italy, Roma: Piazza del Campidoglio has three main Palazzi. Palazzo Senatorio (back, now Rome's city hall), built around 1250-1350 atop the Tabularium (78 BC, housed the archives of the ancient Rome), re-used blocks from the Tabularium, and was modified by Michelangelo around 1535. The Palazzo dei Conservatori (right) was built around 1550, for the local magistrate, on top of a temple (about 550 BC) dedicated to Jupiter "Maximus Capitolinus". Michelangelo's renovation of it incorporated many new architectural ideas. Palazzo Nuovo (left) was built around 1650, based on Michelangelo's ideas, with an identical exterior design to the Palazzo dei Conservatori, which it faces across the piazza. The Capitoline Museums are inside all these three Palazzi surrounding the Piazza del Campidoglio, and interlinked by an underground gallery beneath the piazza. Until around 1475, the main market of the city of Rome was held on and around the Piazza del Campidoglio, while cattle continued to be taxed and sold in the ancient forum located just to the south. Michelangelo Buonarroti (1475 – 1564) had a key role in the design and updating of the Piazza del Campidoglio and its surrounding Palazzi.

## In Region R0: from Paris (France) to N'Djamena (Chad)

- The sub-region R00 will have the capitals Paris (France) and Niamey (Niger) – assistance from Magdeburg (Germany).
- The sub-region R01 will have the capitals Brussels (Belgium) and Porto-Novo (Benin) - assistance from Toronto (Canada).
- The sub-region R02 will have the capitals Amsterdam (Netherlands) and Algiers (Algeria) - assistance from Graz (Austria).
- The sub-region R03 will have the capitals Luxembourg (Luxembourg) and Sao Tome (Sao Tome and Principe) - assistance from Adelaide (Australia).
- The sub-region R04 will have the capitals of Abuja (Nigeria) and Bochum (Germany) - assistance from Nikko (Japan).
- The sub-region R05 will have the capitals Malabo (Equatorial Guinea), Zürich (Switzerland) - assistance from Leeds (UK).
- The sub-region R06 will have the capitals Oslo (Norway) and Tunis (Tunisia) - assistance from Sheffield (UK).
- The sub-region R07 will have the capitals Roma (Italy) and Luanda (Angola) - assistance from Yamagata (Japan).
- The sub-region R08 will have the capitals in Berlin (Germany) and Tripoli (Libya) - assistance from New York (USA).
- The sub-region R09 will have the capitals Prague (Czech Republic) and N'Djamena (Chad) - assistance from Brisbane (Australia).

Japan: In Shinjuku, from the 45<sup>th</sup> fl., 202 m, of Tokyo Met. Gov Blg South Tower): part of the North Tower of Tokyo Met. Gov Blg (243 m, 48 fl, 1991, left), Shinjuku Sumitomo Bldg (210 m, 52 fl, 1974, center), Shinjuku Mitsui Building (224 m, 55 floors, 1974, right).

## In Region R1: from Zagreb (Croatia) to Bujumbura (Burundi)

- The sub-region R10 will have the capitals in Zagreb (Croatia) and Brazzaville (Congo) - assistance from Nantes (France).
- The sub-region R11 will have the capitals in Vienna (Austria), Windhoek (Namibia) - assistance from Bilbao (Spain).
- The sub-region R12 will have the capitals in Stockholm (Sweden), Bangui (Central African Republic) - assistance from Florence (Italy).
- The sub-region R13 will have the capitals in Budapest (Hungary), Rundu (Namibia) - assistance from Monaco (Monaco).
- The sub-region R14 will have the capitals in Belgrade (Serbia), Kananga (Democratic Republic of Congo) - assistance from Liverpool (UK).
- The sub-region R15 will have the capitals in Athens (Greece), Mongu (Zambia) - assistance from Los Angeles (CA, USA).
- The sub-region R16 will have the capitals in Helsinki (Finland) and Gaborone (Botswana) - assistance from Montreal (Canada).
- The sub-region R17 will have the capitals in Bucharest (Romania) and Gaborone (Botswana) - assistance from Philadelphia (PA, USA).
- The sub-region R18 will have the capitals in Minsk (Belarus) and Maseru (Lesotho) - assistance from Orleans (France).
- The sub-region R19 will have the capitals in Chisinau (Republic of Moldova) and Bujumbura (Burundi) - assistance from Hamburg (Germany).

UK, London: At the east end of Westminster Bridge (1862, 250 m, width 26 m, 7 spans, right) over Thames (flowing left to right), Palace of Westminster (1016, 1870, 300 m river front façade, 1,100 rooms, center left, with Victoria Tower (1858, 98 m, left), and Central Tower (91 m)), Big Ben (Elizabeth Tower, 1855, 96 m, center right).

USA, 30 km northwest of Boston: 15 Oct 2008, nice flowers and colors of the trees, in the autumn.

USA, Cambridge: 23 Sep 2009, from Memorial Drive, looking northwest to the MIT (MASSACHVSETTS INSTITVTE OF TECHNOLOGY (in Latin style, with V for U)), MCMXVI (1916).

## In Region R2: from Kiev (Ukraine) to Baghdad (Iraq)

- The sub-region R20 will have the capitals in Kiev (Ukraine) and Kigali (Rwanda) - assistance from Ottawa (Canada).
- The sub-region R21 will have the capitals in Ankara (Turkey) and Khartoum (Sudan) - assistance from Salzburg (Austria).
- The sub-region R22 will have the capitals in Lilongwe (Malawi) and Nicosia (Cyprus) - assistance from Dallas (TX, USA).
- The sub-region R23 will have the capitals in Jerusalem (Israel) and Dodoma (Tanzania) - assistance from Strasbourg (France).
- The sub-region R24 will have the capitals in Damascus (Syria) and Nairobi (Kenya) - assistance from Stuttgart (Germany).
- The sub-region R25 will have the capitals in Krasnodar (Russia) and Addis Ababa (Ethiopia) - assistance from Marseille (France).
- The sub-region R26 will have the capitals in Rostov-on-Don (Russia) and Asmara (Eritrea) - assistance from Leipzig (Germany).
- The sub-region R27 will have the capitals in Stavropol (Russia) and Djibouti (Djibouti) - assistance from Zürich (Switzerland).
- The sub-region R28 will have the capitals in Mosul (Iraq) and Moroni (Comoros) - assistance from Linz (Austria).
- The sub-region R29 will have the capitals in Yerevan (Armenia) and Baghdad (Iraq) - assistance from Göttingen (Germany).

Japan: Mount Fuji (3,776 m, 1707 last eruption) seen from Kawaguchi city (down), near Kawaguchiko (Lake Kawaguchi, 6 km$^2$, 830 m elevation, has an island), 100 km south-west of Tokyo.

Mount Fuji (Fuji-san) is Japan's highest and most important mountain, from physical, cultural and spiritual point of view. The almost perfectly symmetrical cone of Mount Fuji is a symbol of Japan, and a frequent subject of Japanese art. The Japanese artist Katsushika Hokusai (1760 – 1849), born in Edo (now Tokyo) is the author of the woodblock print series 'Thirty six Views of Mount Fuji' (circa 1831) and 'One Hundred Views of Mount Fuji'.

Mount Fuji has appeared in the Japanese literature for many centuries. The summit has been considered to be a sacred place since ancient times. Mount Fuji is located on the main island Honshu, and is visible from Tokyo on a clear day, being covered by snow for half of the year. Because of its high altitude, the weather around Mount Fuji changes very quickly, and clouds are often moving across the peak, obscuring the view from time to time.

The best views of Mount Fuji are from the Fuji-Hakone-Izu National Park, near one of the five lakes that surround Mount Fuji: Kawaguchiko (Lake Kawaguchi), Lake Motosu (140 m deep), Saiko (Lake Sai, known as the Western Lake), Shojiko (Lake Shoji is the smallest), and Lake Yamanaka (the largest and easternmost, is also the third highest lake in Japan, at 980 m elevation).

London: On Gagarin (First Man in Space) Terrace, on the southwest part of the South Building (1899) of the Royal Observatory Greenwich (1676), looking northeast to the south part of the west side (right), the west part of the south side (left), and to the statue of Yuri Gagarin (1934-1968, Russian cosmonaut, the first man to journey into space, with Vostok spacecraft, which completed an orbit (1h 48') of the Earth on 12 April 1961. Resting place: Kremlin Wall Necropolis).

## In Region R3: from Riyadh (Saudi Arabia) to Malé (Maldives)

- The sub-region R30 will have the capitals in Riyadh (Saudi Arabia) and Mogadishu (Somalia) - assistance from Bonn (Germany).
- The sub-region R31 will have the capitals in Baku (Azerbaijan) and Antananarivo (Madagascar) - assistance from Le Mans (France).
- The sub-region R32 will have the capitals in Oral (Kazakhstan) and Tehran (Iran) - assistance from Pisa (Italy).
- The sub-region R33 will have the capitals in Ashgabat (Turkmenistan) and Abu Dhabi (United Arab Emirates) - assistance from Wolfsburg (Germany).
- The sub-region R34 will have the capitals in Magnitogorsk (Russia) and Muscat (Oman) - assistance from Toulouse (France).
- The sub-region R35 will have the capitals in Chelyabinsk (Russia) and Herat (Afghanistan) - assistance from Basel (Switzerland).
- The sub-region R36 will have the capitals in Tyumen (Russia) and Kandahar (Afghanistan) - assistance from Nagoya (Japan).
- The sub-region R37 will have the capitals in Dushanbe (Tajikistan) and Labytnangi (Russia) - assistance from Limoges (France).
- The sub-region R38 will have the capitals in Astana (Kazakhstan) and Kabul (Afghanistan) - assistance from Rostock (Germany).
- The sub-region R39 will have the capitals in Islamabad (Pakistan) and Malé (Maldives) - assistance from La Rochelle (France).

France, Paris: Tour Eiffel (1889, 324 m, 279 m at the 3rd level, looking north-west): Tour Eiffel shadow (center), Pont d'Iéna over La Seine (left down), Avenue de New York (green, on the north side of La Seine), Jardin du Trocadéro (1878, 1937, with the Fountain of Warsaw (center left)), Palais de Chaillot (center up), Port de Suffren (down left), Port de la Bourdonnais (down right), Ave. d'Eylau (up-left, vertical), Av. Albert de Mun (center right).

## In Region R4: from Bishkek (Kyrgyzstan) to Brahmapur (India)

- The sub-region R40 will have the capitals in Bishkek (Kyrgyzstan) and Jaipur (India) - assistance from Osaka (Japan).
- The sub-region R41 will have the capitals in Akola (India) and Kashgar (China) - assistance from Genoa (Italy).
- The sub-region R42 will have the capitals in Almaty (Kazakhstan) and Coimbatore (India) - assistance from Perth (Australia).
- The sub-region R43 will have the capitals in Kuybyshev (Russia) and Agra (India) - assistance from Fukuoka (Japan).
- The sub-region R44 will have the capitals in Vertikos (Russia) and Nagpur (India) - assistance from Coral Bay (Australia).
- The sub-region R45 will have the capitals in Chennai (India) and Colombo (Sri Lanka) - assistance from Sapporo (Japan).
- The sub-region R46 will have the capitals in Lucknow (India) and Fedosikha (Russia) - assistance from Niigata (Japan).
- The sub-region R47 will have the capitals in Bilaspur (India) and Kolpashevo (Russia) - assistance from Albany (Australia).
- The sub-region R48 will have the capitals in Visakhapatnam (India) and Barnaul (Russia) - assistance from Hiroshima (Japan).
- The sub-region R49 will have the capitals in Brahmapur (India) and Tomsk (Russia) - assistance from Yokohama (Japan).

UK, London: From the Bridge Street, at the northwest corner of Big Ben, looking south to the northwest garden (right) and entrances (left and back) of the Palace of Westminster (1016).

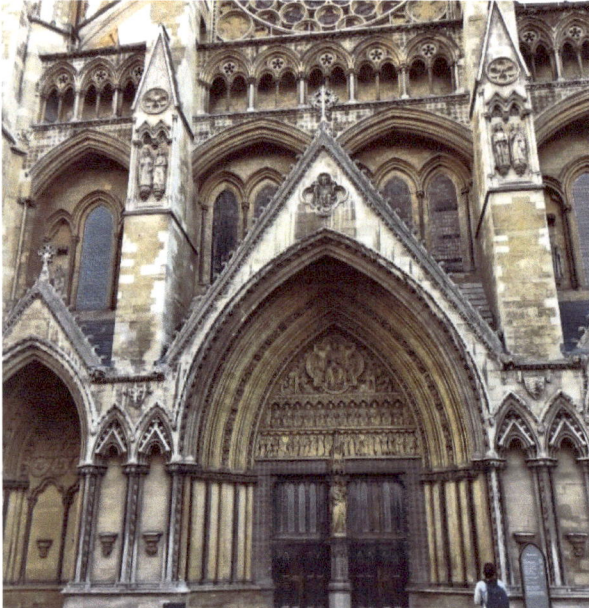

Detail of the north entrance of Westminster Abbey (960, 1517, Collegiate Church of St Peter at Westminster, Anglican abbey hosting daily services, and every coronation since 1066, tower height 69 m, floor area 3,000 m$^2$).

## In Region R5: from Kathmandu (Nepal) to Dehong (China)

- The sub-region R50 will have the capitals in Kathmandu (Nepal) and Patna (India) - assistance from Kobe (Japan).
- The sub-region R51 will have the capitals in Bayingol (China) and Novokuznetsk (Russia) - assistance from Vichy (France).
- The sub-region R52 will have the capitals in Thimphu (Bhutan) and Dhaka (Bangladesh) - assistance from Jena (Germany).
- The sub-region R53 will have the capitals in Lhasa (China) and Achinsk (Russia) - assistance from Reims (France).
- The sub-region R54 will have the capitals in Abakan (Russia) and Kumul (China) - assistance from Fribourg (Switzerland).
- The sub-region R55 will have the capitals in Kyzyl (Russia) and Dibrugarh (India) - assistance from Denmark (Australia).
- The sub-region R56 will have the capitals in Bassein (Myanmar) and Tinsukia (India) - assistance from Chiba (Japan).
- The sub-region R57 will have the capitals in Yushu City (China) and Tinskoy (Russia) - assistance from Klagenfurt (Austria).
- The sub-region R58 will have the capitals in Jiuquan (China) and Medan (Indonesia) - assistance from Lucerne (Switzerland).
- The sub-region R59 will have the capitals in Chiang Mai (Thailand) and Dehong (China) - assistance from Mulhouse (France).

France, Paris: The statue Cérès ou L'Été (1726) by Coustou Guillaume Lyon (1677 – 1746) , placed in 1735 on the east side of the Basin Octogonal in Jardin des Tuileries (created in 1564 as the garden of Palais des Tuileries (1564 – 1883, which was located between le Pavillion de Marsan, at the west end of the north part of Musée du Louvre, and Pavillon de Flore, at the west end of the south part of Musée du Louvre)).

## In Region R6: from Bangkok (Thailand) to Chita (Russia)

- The sub-region R60 will have the capitals in Bangkok (Thailand) and Kuala Lumpur (Malaysia) - assistance from Besançon (France).
- The sub-region R61 will have the capitals in Vientiane (Laos) and Singapore – assistance from Freiburg im Breisgau (Germany).
- The sub-region R62 will have the capitals in Phnom Penh (Cambodia) and Irkutsk (Russia) – assistance from Baden (Switzerland).
- The sub-region R63 will have the capitals in Palembang (Indonesia), Hanoi (Vietnam) – assistance from Thun (Switzerland).
- The sub-region R64 will have the capitals in Ulan Bator (Mongolia) and Ulan-Ude (Russia) – assistance from Chaumont (France).
- The sub-region R65 will have the capitals in Cirebon (Indonesia) and Nanning (China) – assistance from Vaduz (Lichtenstein).
- The sub-region R66 will have the capitals in Pontianak (Indonesia) and Baotou (China) – assistance from Lugano (Switzerland).
- The sub-region R67 will have the capitals in Surakarta (Indonesia) and Yichang (China) – assistance from Thonon-les-Bain (France).
- The sub-region R68 will have the capitals in Surabaya (Indonesia) and Changsha (China) – assistance from Burgdorf (Switzerland).
- The sub-region R69 will have the capitals in Chita (Russia) and Hong Kong (China) – assistance from Colmar (France).

UK, London: From a bridge over St James's Park Lake, looking west to the northeast façade of the Buckingham Palace (1703, 1850, 1913).

From the northwest corner of Trafalgar Square (1840), looking northeast to The National Gallery (1824, over 2,300 paintings, left), St. Martin in the Fields Church (1724, right, with music recitals.

## In Region R7: from Nanchang (China) to Melbourne (Australia)

- The sub-region R70 will have the capitals in Bandar Seri Begawan (Brunei Darussalam) and Nanchang (China) – assistance from Turku (Finland).
- The sub-region R71 will have the capitals in Krasnokamensk (Russia) and Jinan (China) – assistance from St. Gallen (Switzerland).
- The sub-region R72 will have the capitals in Baguio City (Philippines) and Hangzhou (China) – assistance from Dole (France).
- The sub-region R73 will have the capitals in Manila (Philippines) and Taipei (Taiwan, China) – assistance from Metz (France).
- The sub-region R74 will have the capitals in Kupang (Indonesia) and Shanghai (China) – assistance from Davos (Switzerland).
- The sub-region R75 will have the capitals in Pyongyang (North Korea) and Seoul (South Korea) – assistance from Versailles (France).
- The sub-region R76 will have the capitals in Vladivostok (Russia) and Busan (South Korea) – assistance from Innsbruck (Austria).
- The sub-region R77 will have the capitals in Kyoto (Japan) and Khabarovsk (Russia) – assistance from Germering (Germany).
- The sub-region R78 will have the capitals in Nagoya (Japan) and Komsomolsk-on-Amur (Russia) – assistance from Venice (Italy).
- The sub-region R79 will have the capitals in Sendai (Japan) and Melbourne (Australia) – assistance from St. Moritz (Switzerland).

Japan: In Shinjuku, Shinjuku Center Building (223 m, 54 fl, 1979, left), Mode Gakuen Cocoon Tower (204 m, 50 floors, 2008, center), Keio Plaza Hotel North Tower (180 m, 47 fl, 1971, right).

## In Region R8: from Anchorage (Alaska, USA) to Lima (Peru)

- The sub-region R80 will have the capitals in Uelen (Russia) and Anchorage (Alaska, USA), – assistance from Zug (Switzerland).
- The sub-region R81 will have the capitals in Vancouver (Canada) and San Jose (CA, USA) – assistance from Odense (Denmark).
- The sub-region R82 will have the capitals in Vernon (Canada) and Los Angeles (CA, USA) – assistance from Amstetten (Austria).
- The sub-region R83 will have the capitals in Calgary (Canada) and Tijuana (Mexico) – assistance from Chur (Switzerland).
- The sub-region R84 will have the capitals in Hermosillo (Mexico) and Tucson (AR, USA) – assistance from Bergen (Norway).
- The sub-region R85 will have the capitals in Chihuahua (Mexico) and Regina (Canada) – assistance from Gothenburg (Sweden).
- The sub-region R86 will have the capitals in San Luis Potosi City (Mexico) and Winnipeg (Canada) – assistance from Yverdon-les-Bains (Switzerland).
- The sub-region R87 will have the capitals in Tulsa (OK, USA) and Veracruz (Mexico) – assistance from Bregenz (Austria).
- The sub-region R88 will have the capitals in Memphis (TN, USA) and San José (Costa Rica) – assistance from Uppsala (Sweden).
- The sub-region R89 will have the capitals in Lima (Peru) and Boston (MA, USA) – assistance from Tampere (Finland).

France, Paris: The north-west and south-west sides of the Tour Eiffel (1889, 324 m) with the north (pilier nord, left, has an elevator (1986)), west (center) and south (right) legs. Work on the foundations started on 28 January 1887. Those for the east and south (right) legs had each leg resting on four 2 m concrete slabs; for the other two, each slab has two piles 15 m long and 6 m in diameter, to a depth of 22 m to support the concrete slabs 6 m thick.

## In Region R9: from La Paz (Bolivia) to London (United Kingdom)

- The sub-region R90 will have the capitals in La Paz (Bolivia) and Bangor (Maine, USA) – assistance from Aosta (Italy).
- The sub-region R91 will have the capitals in Caracas (Venezuela) and Road Town (British Virgin Islands) – assistance from Obergoms (Switzerland).
- The sub-region R92 will have the capitals in Buenos Aires (Argentina) and Fort-de-France (Martinique) – assistance from Freudenstadt (Germany).
- The sub-region R93 will have the capitals in Asuncion (Paraguay) and Montevideo (Uruguay) – assistance from Winterthur (Switzerland).
- The sub-region R94 will have the capitals in Cayenne (French Guiana), St. John's (Canada) – assistance from Novara (Italy).
- The sub-region R95 will have the capitals in Rio de Janeiro (Brazil) and Dakar (Senegal) – assistance from Toyama (Japan).
- The sub-region R96 will have the capitals in Freetown (Sierra Leone) and Lisbon (Portugal) – assistance from Kawasaki (Japan).
- The sub-region R97 will have the capitals in Bamako (Mali) and Athlone (Ireland) – assistance from Ulm (Germany).
- The sub-region R98 will have the capitals in Yamoussoukro (Cote d'Ivoire) and Madrid (Spain) – assistance from Okayama (Japan).
- The sub-region R99 will have the capitals in Ouagadougou (Burkina Faso) and London (United Kingdom) - assistance from Vaasa (Finland).

UK, London: On Thames looking northeast to the northeast half of The Tower Bridge (1886-1894, bascule/suspension bridge, height 65 m, 244 m).

London: On Thames looking north to Oliver's Wharf, a luxury residential building on Wapping High Street, parallel to the river.

## 5.4. Level 3 Management: Ten L3 friendly managers

Ten L3 friendly managers for the 10 regions, who will supervise and assist the 10 L2 managers of the 10 sub-regions of each region, for a total of about 770,000,000 people for each region.

- The Region R0 will have the first capitals in Bern (Switzerland) and Libreville (Gabon) – assistance from Oxford (UK). For better quality and consistency of the management, we'll have the first two cities from the region R0, and the third city from outside. Actually, being inside the same country Terra, any city, sub-region or region can ask for advice or help from anybody.

- The Region R1 will have the first capitals in Warsaw (Poland) and Pretoria (South Africa) – assistance from Miami (FL, USA).

- The Region R2 will have the first capitals in Moscow (Russia) and Cairo (Egypt) – assistance from Grenoble (France).

- The Region R3 will have the first capitals in Astana (Kazakhstan) and Karachi (Pakistan), – assistance from Montpellier (France).

- The Region R4 will have the first capitals in New Delhi (India) and Novosibirsk (Russia) – assistance from Magdeburg (Germany).

- The Region R5 will have the first capitals in Krasnoyarsk (Russia) and Urumqi (China) – assistance from Avignon (France).

- The Region R6 will have the first capitals in Jakarta (Indonesia) and Beijing (China) – assistance from Neuchâtel (Switzerland).

- The Region R7 will have the first capitals in Tokyo (Japan) and Sydney (Australia) – assistance from Malmö (Sweden).

Italy, Verona: 28 Sep 2008, International Festival with Scottish Bagpipers in Piazza Bra, Verona (Roman Colonia in 89 BC, municipium 49 BC).

France, Paris: The south-east of la Tour Eiffel (1889, 324 m including the antenna at the top; without the antenna, it is 300 m), seen from Place Jacques Rueff in Jardin du Champ de Mars.

- The Region R8 will have the first capitals in Washington (USA) and Mexico City (Mexico) – assistance from Bellinzona (Switzerland).

- The Region R9 will have the first capitals in Halifax (Canada) and Brasilia (Brazil) – assistance from Biel (Switzerland).

Italy, Venice: Palazzo Giustinian (left), Piazza San Marco (center), Palazzo Ducale (center-right), seen from the east end of Canal Grande.

## 5.5. Level 4 Management: very friendly 10 Advisers

5.5.1 - L4 very friendly 10 Advisers of the world, who will supervise and assist the 10 L3 managers of the 10 regions of the Earth, for a total of about 7,700,000,000 people – all the people on Earth, citizens of Peaceful Terra.

5.5.2 - The L4 very friendly 10 Advisers of the world will be located each in one the ten Regions R0, R1,…, R9. For example, in the beginning, for the first month (then changing every month), the ten Advisers of the world will be located:

- in R0: Barcelona (Spain)
- in R1: Benghazi (Libya)
- in R2: Addis Ababa (Ethiopia)
- in R3: Hyderabad (Pakistan)
- in R4: Bhopal (India)
- in R5: Mandalay (Myanmar)
- in R6: Nanchong (China)
- in R7: Khabarovsk (Russia)
- in R8: Houston (USA)
- in R9: Recife (Brazil)

5.5.3 – These ten L4 Advisers will be in permanent contact with each other, and with the L3 Advisers, for the best management of the world.

5.5.4 – The ten L4 Advisers will work by consensus only.

5.5.5 - The ten L4 Advisers will be elected from the 10 regions, and each of them will be the First Adviser (**First among equals** – from Latin: Primus inter pares) for one month, by rotation.

5.5.6 - The First Adviser only coordinates the work of the other 9 Advisors for one month.

Paris: East of Louvre: Place du Louvre, the north tower (1860, with a bell called "Marie", center) of l'Église Saint-Germain l'Auxerrois (founded around 650, rebuilt many times, with a porch which has a rose window, and a balustrade above which encircles the whole church, from 1439, right), and la Mairie du 1er Arrondissment (1859, left). Inside the church are a 15th-century wooden statue of Saint Germain, and a stone carved statue of Saint-Vincent.

5.5.7 – The ten L4 Advisers will move each month from a first capital of a region to the second capital of another region, at random (or based on urgency, if an emergency occurred). This mobility is essential for having a long period of tranquility and harmony.

5.5.8 - The First Adviser, on the last day of each month, will present in writing for the world (no more than 5 standard pages) a clear and precise Monthly World Report, with a list of finished and unfinished tasks.

5.5.9 - The other 9 Advisers will add their comments to the Monthly World Report (no more than half a page each - total report less than 9.5 pages).

5.5.10 - The top 10 Advisers will manage Police and all other Departments.

5.5.11 - For obvious uncooperative or improper attitude of one top Advisor X, the other 9 can replace X with X's number 2, and X will receive appropriate medical treatment.

5.5.12 - When vacancies happen for Advisors, the number 2 for those Advisors will fill the vacancies.

5.5.13 - All the activities of all Advisors will be recorded in computers and videos, and on paper, for people to be able to see what they are doing.

5.5.14 - Advisors at all levels should work 40 hours/week, with 4 weeks vacation, but many services (medical, police (firemen should be part of the police), emergency, volunteers) should be non-stop.

5.5.15 – Advisors' compensation should be the world annual average salary (in 2019 less than $10,000) plus 4% of that world average salary, for level 4 (total $10,400), + 3 % for level 3, and so on. They all should work to increase the world average salary, in order to get themselves an increase.

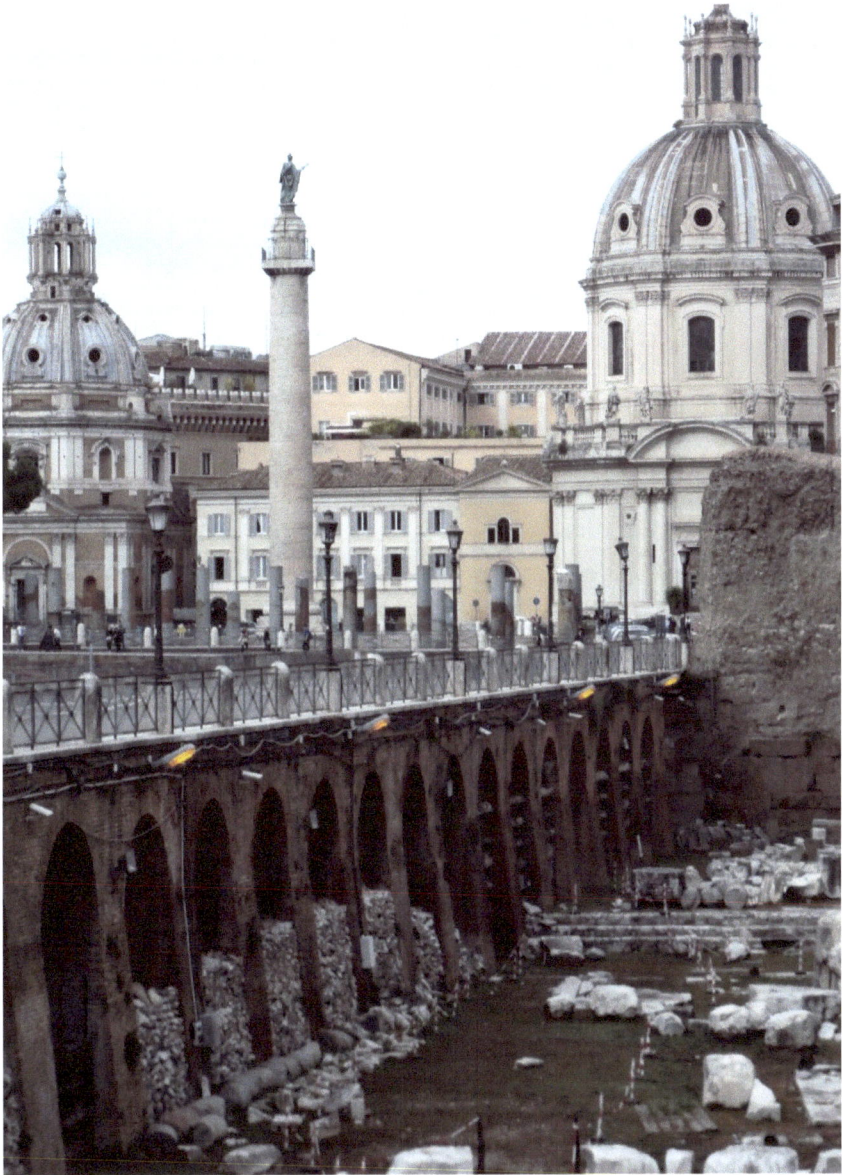

Italy, Rome. Down: a part of Forum Augustum (2 BC). Back: a part of Forum Traiani (113 AD), including Columna Traiani (113, center back), with a band (180 m) of carved reliefs, which winds around the Trajan's Column, describing Trajan's Dacian war campaigns (101-102 and 105-106 AD). After Trajan's death, his 6 m statue was on top until 1587. His ashes and later those of his wife Plotina were placed in the base of the column.

5.5.16 - All the other world government employees will have a compensation close to the average compensation of the people in the area where they are located.

5.5.17 - All Advisors are free to speak about their administrative work, with modesty.

5.5.18 - All spending proposals from Advisers must be approved by their 5 assistants (doctors, mathematicians, CEOs, engineers and teachers), and must have an already existing funding in the budget.

5.5.19 - Advisors (and all the others) cannot declare war, reprisals or capture land or water.

5.5.20 - Advisors (and all the others) cannot raise and support armies, navy, or any military forces.

5.5.21 - At least 7 of the top 10 Advisers should be present every working day.

5.5.22 - The Advisors will be located in the current government buildings, and the excess government buildings and properties will be sold, in order to increase the budget, and to reduce the expenses.

5.5.23 - In order to better know the world government, to help it, and, especially, to improve it, all able people of the world will work as volunteers at least one day per year in each of the seven departments.

5.5.24 - After each Monthly World Report, a public opinion survey about the report should be taken, and presented to all Advisors.

5.5.25 - All activities of the Advisors, and others from the small World Government, will be available to the people on a website.

5.5.26 - The top 10 Advisers (and all the others) will collaborate via e-mail, telephone, videoconferences, mail, or face to face, when needed, to produce practical results for all people, very fast.

Italy, Venice: Palazzo Molin (right) on Fondamenta Zattere Al Ponte Lungo, on the north bank of Canale della Giudecca, south of Venice.

## 5.6. Five Assistants

5.6.1 - Each Advisor, and each manager at all levels, will have 5 immediate assistants:
1) a mathematician for finance and all other calculations,
2) a medical doctor for keeping everybody healthy, calm, polite, friendly and optimist,
3) a CEO for good management,
4) an engineer for all practical projects, and
5) a teacher for education, training and related areas.

5.6.2 – The five assistants play a key role, because they are highly qualified professionals, who actually will carry on the practical management of the world.

5.6.3 - The five assistants' integrity, professionalism and friendliness will significantly improve the quality of the world and local governments.

5.6.4 - The five assistants are really the experts. They will assist the Advisors and all levels of management, in order to have an efficient, correct and professional working of the world government at all levels.

France, Paris: Tour Eiffel (1889, 324 m, 279 m at the 3rd level, looking south-east): Tour Eiffel's east leg (down left) and south leg (down right), Jardin du Champ de Mars, Avenue Anatole France (center left), Allée Adrienne Lecouvreur (next left), Avenue Pierre Loti (center right), Allée Thomy Thierry (next right), Avenue Charles Floquet (next right, after the first row of buildings), Avenue de Suffren (next right), Avenue Gustave Eiffel (down, with busses)..

## 5.7. The Honorific World Observer

5.7.1 - A Honorific World Observer will be quietly elected by direct vote – starting, for example, 1st September 2022 - for only one 3 years term, with the main duty to observe that the top 10 Advisers efficiently perform their duties, and keep their words – if they don't, they will be changed.

5.7.2 - For managers and for everybody else, keeping their word is a serious and strict requirement.

5.7.3 - The Honorific World Observer has this responsibility for the top 10 Advisors, but all people will pay attention to this. Words must become again important and respected.

USA: The George Washington Bridge (1962, 1450 m, spanning Hudson River from New York City to Fort Lee, New Jersey, with routes 95 and 80, near Exit 73 for Fort Lee and route 67.

London: Inside (southwest) the British Museum (1753). Head of the Egyptian pharaoh Amenhotep III (1411 BC – 1353 BC (age 58), pharaoh for 33 years (1386 BC (age 25) – 1353 BC), Egyptian Amana-Hatpa meaning god Amun is Satisfied, also known as Amenhotep the Magnificent, the 9th pharaoh of the 18th Dynasty (1570 BC – 1293 BC)) wearing the red crown of Lower Egypt, Amana period at the end of the 18th Dynasty, 1360 BC, from Thebes. One of his grandsons was Tutankhamun (1342 BC – 1323 BC (age 19)).

## 5.8. Small World Government with 7 Departments

5.8.1 - All the employees of the World Government are temporary, and must reapply for their positions every year.

5.8.2 – There is no need for unions.

5.8.3 - The World Government will be limited to:
1) the Office of the Honorific Observer (less than 10 employees),
2) the Office of the top ten Advisors (less than 100 employees), and
3) 7 small departments.

5.8.4 - The World Government will have these 7 small departments:

Italy, Roma: Forum Romanum (80 BC, right), Temple of Saturn 42 BC, center, Arch of Severus 203, center-left, Temple of Vespasian 80, left

## - Tax Department

- Collects taxes of 15% of the income of people and revenue of companies.

- The Manager of the Tax Department is appointed for a three-year term by the World 10 Advisers.

- The number of employees must be under 50,000, with excellent computers, and advanced software.

Finland, Helsinki: a commercial harbor in the south-west of the city, near Hietalahdenranta, with the boat Aranda.

## - Treasury

Treasury will control all the financial issues, including:
- antitrust
- fiscal service
- financial cooperation
- financing bank
- world reserve system
- world budget using only revenue, no borrowing, and spending only on strict necessary needs
– all the budgets, at all levels, will have a 2% surplus, which will be returned to the taxpayers
- register of all government papers and activities
- archives and records
- assist all people to have savings accounts for old age (the old age will be starting around 70), and 10% of their income should automatically go to their savings accounts. For those unable to work, their doctors and mathematicians will decide case by case.
- bankruptcies, in general, will be discouraged, and when strict necessary, will be analyzed and solved, case by case, by the doctors, mathematicians and CEOs who worked with the people who asked the bankruptcy.
- encourage all families to assist their parents, grandparents, and great-grandparents.
- housing finance
- housing for all people
- no homelessness
- consumer financial protection
- pensions
- privacy
- current social security until replaced by personal savings
- personnel management
- general services for the world government
- each the 10 regions will receive 2.5% of the world taxes - at least 30% of the money will be sent to villages and cities.
- each of the 100 sub-regions will receive 0.25% of the world taxes. At least 40% of the money will be sent to villages and cities.

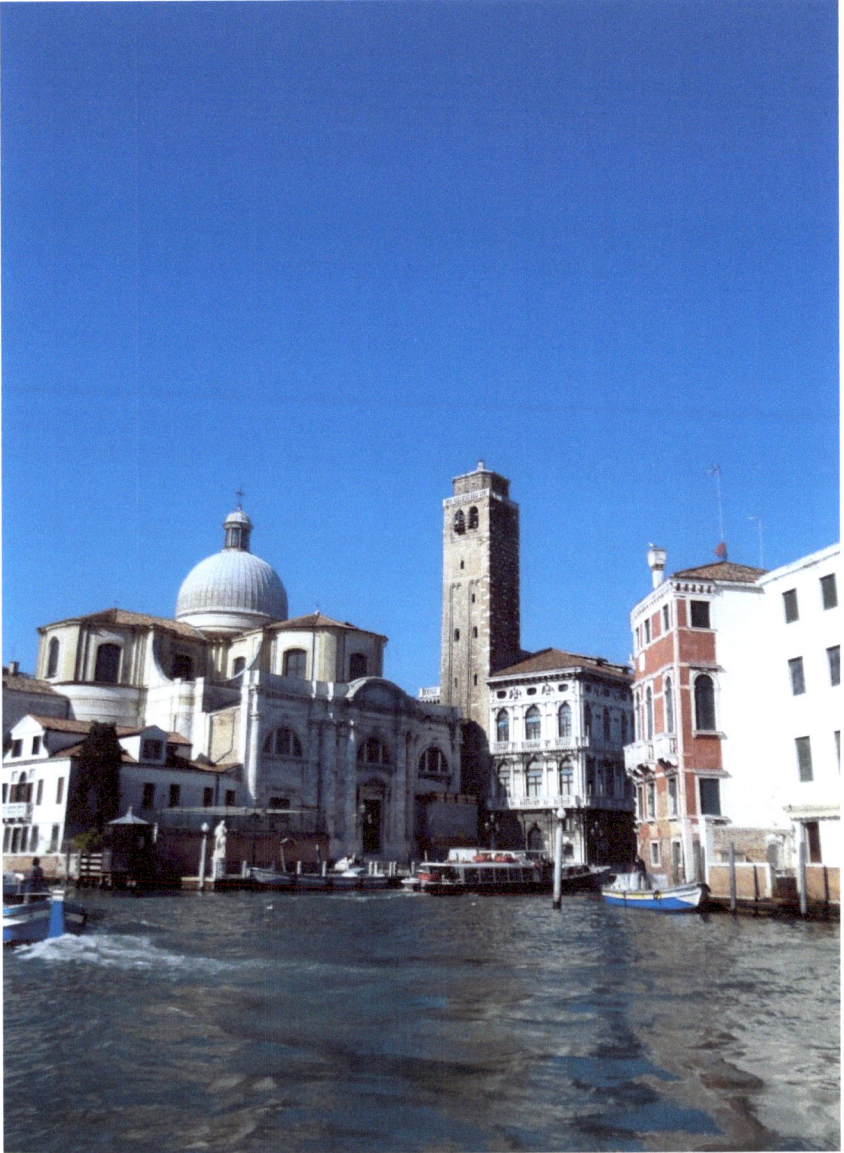

Italy, Venice: Palazzo Querini (right), Canale di Cannaregio (center-right), Palazzo Labia (center-right), Chiesa San Geremia (center-left), 350 m east from the Venice Santa Lucia Train Station, 1.3 km from the west end of the Canal, and 2.6 km from Piazza San Marco.

- The World Central Bank will include all current central banks – starting, for example, on May 1st, 2023.
- The Special Credit Card (SCC) will be issued by the World Central Bank.
- Advisors will create a new world currency, named, for example, "coin", and all the other currencies will be exchanged for coins. The World Central Bank will implement the details.
- The counterfeiting and all other bad things, which some sick people do, will be medically treated (in specialized medical institutions when necessary), and those who did bad things will pay all the expenses, and will reimburse the victims. Victims will always be very protected, and helped to recover the losses from the attackers.

USA, Washington (1790), National Archives and Records Administration building (1935), on Constitution Avenue.

From the Bow Street, the northeast façade of the Royal Opera House at Covent Garden (1732, 1808, 1858, 1999, capacity 2,256). In 1734, Covent Garden presented its first ballet, Pygmalion. On 14 January 1947, the Covent Garden Opera Company gave its first performance of Carmen (1875, opera in four acts, based on a novella of the same title by Prosper Mérimée (1803-1870 (age 67))) by French composer Georges Bizet (1838-1875 (age 36)).

## - People Assistance Department

It will assist people in general, including:
- parent assistance
- dispute resolution
- in very simple disputes or culpa levis (ordinary negligence, like late payments, etc.), one single assistant will decide within minutes, and all people will go back to work
- census very 5 years
- election assistance every 20 months
 - special credit cards
- people protection against abuses from anybody
- completely eliminate corruption, organized crime and drug trafficking
- all people in the world will remain in their places, and the improvements will come to them. Those who want to move to other places, will need first a special invitation from at least 10 people (not family related) where they want to move.
- all the Tribunals and related areas will be transformed in people assistance services, based on friendliness, collaboration and goodwill.
- It is well understood that no excessive bail will be required, no excessive fines imposed, no cruel and unusual punishments applied, but, at the same time, it is well understood that a person who did a bad thing will receive the necessary corrective medical treatment, and will reimburse all people who suffered damages, and the medical treatment. The victims will always receive special attention.
- Nobility (King, Prince, etc.) could continue to exist in some places, but they should not interfere with activities of the Advisors, and actually should help them.
- food safety
- trash & recycling
- free commerce
- jobs assistance
- postal service
- labor safety and harmonious relations
- land, water

- volunteers
- fitness, sport, tourism
- 10 world holidays: the normal 4 Earth events (2 solstices (around 21 June, around 21 December), and 2 equinoxes (around 21 March, around 21 September), Mother's Day on 1$^{st}$ May, Father's Day on 6 August, Children's Day on 6 November, Grandparents' Day on 6 February, and 2 optional days (like Thanksgiving or a Religious Day (Christmas), and New Year).

Japan, Inzai Post Office, 300 m north-est from the entrance to the Inzai (Chiba) campus of Tokyo Denki University (TDU, founded in 1907) in Muzai-Gakuendai, 34 km north-east of Tokyo.

France, Paris: The Panthéon (1758 - 1790, 83 m height, mausoleum in the Latin Quarter in Paris, modeled on the Pantheon in Rome), seen from the west end of Rue Soufflot, near Jardin du Luxembourg (1612). This mausoleum, with the motto: *Aux grands hommes, la patrie reconnaissante* ("To the great men, the grateful homeland"), contains the remains of distinguished French citizens (Voltaire, Rousseau, Victor Hugo, etc.). In 1851, physicist Léon Foucault demonstrated the rotation of the earth by his experiment conducted in the Panthéon, by constructing a 67 m Foucault pendulum beneath the central dome.

## - Medical Department

It will manage all medical and healthcare related areas, including:
- human services
- conflict resolution
- families, children, elderly
- medicine approval
- disease control and prevention
- medical doctors and assistants will make regular home visits, at least once a year, to all people, to keep them healthy, and to prevent illnesses.
- medical research: cancer, heart, lung, blood, arthritis, surgical robotics, connected computers for healthcare, etc.
- healthy homes, streets, stores, working places, etc.
- healthy aging
- all misunderstandings, disagreements or conflicts of any nature will be treated by medical personnel (with police help when strict necessary), until all is back to normal.
- no prisons are necessary, only specialized medical institutions (in simple cases, the places where the treated people live can be used, with the necessary limitations and surveillance)
- If a person X is considered that did a bad thing, X will have, within 3 days, a discussion with one or more doctors and other assistants, and will be informed of the nature and cause of the bad thing; including witnesses against and for him. Then a decision will be taken within other 3 days, by a group of doctors and other assistants. Victims of bad people will always have priority to discuss their problems with one or more doctors and other assistants, and quick decisions will be taken within 3 days, by a group of doctors and other assistants. Protection of victims has always priority.
- in order to better know the world government, to help it, and, especially, to improve it, all able people of the world will work as volunteers at least one day per year in the local facility of this department, which will have a special office for managing this volunteer work.

– all people will have government medical insurance, and they can also have private medical insurance

– there will be doctors working for the government 100%, or only part-time, or having only private practice, all with reasonable salaries and fees.

– there will be government pharmaceutical institutions and private pharmaceutical companies, offering reasonable priced medicines, without advertising to the general public.

Italy, Venice: Fermata Ferrovia (left), Palazzo Calbo-Crotta (left), Chiesa San Geremia (back), Ponte degli Scalzi (bridge of the barefoot, 1934).

On Broad Ct looking northeast, off Bow Street to the northeast, 50 m north of the Royal Opera House at Covent Garden (1732, 1808, 1858, 1999, capacity 2,256; in 1734, Covent Garden presented its first ballet, Pygmalion), the bronze statue Young Dancer, by the Italian-born (in Mestre, near Venice, in 1921) British sculptor Enzo Plazzotta (1921-1981 (age 60)). To the right up, five red telephone boxes, at 5 Broad Ct, a tourist attraction.

## - Police

Police will provide assistance for:
- accidents
- disasters
- complete elimination of nuclear, chemical and biological arms, firearms and explosives
- world complete security
- world cooperation
- conflict reduction and resolution
- investigations
- emergency assistance
- training
- delinquency prevention in general, and especially juvenile
- protection of Advisors, important government buildings, etc.
- extended surveillance and reconnaissance to prevent bad events
- fire protection
- volunteers to help police
- police will be present at public meetings, services, shows, etc., in order to protect the public
- public order
- ensuring traffic safety
- completely eliminate corruption, organized crime and drug trafficking
- movement of people based on civilized rules
- assist and protect those who have encountered violence
- World Police and specialists from the former United Nations and Interpol will be ready and very mobile for urgent and special operations, when they are needed.
- Police will be the only department which will have some small arms, in order to stop some very bad people (who are very sick).
- a small manufacturing and maintenance of arms unit will be part of the Police Department, under strict control.
- Police will work with medical personnel, mathematicians, CEOs, engineers, teachers and others, to make sure that all the people on

the Planet are in good mental health, in order to prevent bad situations. This is also a major responsibility of all Advisors.
- prevention of bad events
- The Advisors will allocate the necessary budget for Police, and Police will assist people in need.

Italy, Roma: The Arch of Constantine (315, left) and Amphitheatrum Flavium (80 AD, Colosseum, right), from Via di San Gregorio.

London: From Charing Cross Rd, looking southeast to the northwest part of the front part of the English Anglican church St Martin in the Fields (1724, at the northeast corner of Trafalgar Square in the City of Westminster, spire height 59 m, 12 bells, tenor bell weight 1,486 kg, excavations under found a grave from about 410 AD (Roman era), in 1222 there was a church here, in 1542 Henry VIII rebuilt the church, in 1606 James I enlarged the church). It is famous for its regular lunchtime and evening concerts; Academy of St Martin-in-the-Fields performs here, and many other ensembles.

## - Education Department

- Over 2 billions of children in the world will get a solid peace-oriented education, to give a solid peace-oriented foundation for a good, free, peaceful and prosperous life.
- Education is very important – teachers will work with parents and grandparents, to educate the children to leave healthy in a sustainable peace, liberty and prosperity.
- Discipline must be strict, and those who do not behave properly, will get medical assistance.
- The world will have 4 school levels (SLs) of education:
SL1 – Kindergarten – 2 years: age 5 and 6
SL2 – Primary School – 4 years: age 7, 8, 9 and 10
SL3 – Secondary School – 3 years: age 11, 12 and 13
SL4 – High School or Vocational School – 4 years: age 14, 15, 16 and 17
- A World Library will include the Library of Congress and all the other great libraries – they will remain where they are now, but will be digitally interconnected, and accessible from any place in the world.
- adult education: technical, career
- training for employment
- management training
- post high school education
- peace education
- world constitution education

Italy, Venice: In the middle of the west façade of the Basilica di San Marco, the central bronze-fashioned door, in a round-arched portal, encircled by polychrome marble columns. Above this door there are three round bas-relief cycles of Romanesque art. The external cycle above the door surrounds a 19th century gilded mosaic (Last Judgment). A Japanese couple, with their Japanese photographer, make their wedding photographs in this most beautiful place.

France, Paris: Musée du Louvre (1793, in Palais du Louvre (1550)): from Cour Napoléon, the left side of the central part of the western façade of Pavillon de l'Horloge or Pavillon Sully (1624 – 1654, under Kings Louis XIII (1601 – 1643, reign 1610 – 1643), and Louis XIV (1638 – 1715, reign 1643 – 1715)), which is on the east side of Cour Napoléon and of the west side of Cour Carrée (which can be seen through the door).

## - Science & Technology Department.

It will help in the areas of:
- mathematics
- statistics
- science
- technology
- Algorithmic Governance will be an essential tool for a better and impartial governing of the world, used by the Advisers elected by people. Mathematicians from all countries will work to improve the Algorithmic Governance, to better serve the people.
- cyberspace complete security will be achieved and strictly maintained
- information systems
- computer services
- Internet
- scientific cooperation
- economic development at the world level
- infrastructure improvement and maintenance at the world level
- innovation and improvements in all areas, at the world level
- transportation at the world level
- safety
- security
- aviation
- highway
- cars
- railroads without noise
- maritime administration
- logistics
- strategic planning at the world level
- public works
- fleet maintenance
- standards: weights, measures, etc.
- research at the world level
- risk analysis
- laboratories
- engineering

Shinjuku, one of the 23 special wards of Tokyo, with Shinjuku Mitsui Building (224 m, 55 floors, 1974, left), Shinjuku Center Building (223 m, 54 floors, 1979, center), Mode Gakuen Cocoon Tower (204 m, 50 floors, 2008, center-right).

Tokyo started around 1150 as a small fishing village named Edo (which means estuary). Edo was first fortified by the Edo clan, around 1180. In 1457 Edo Castle was built. In 1590 Tokugawa Ieyasu transformed Edo into his base and later, in 1603, the town became the center of his nationwide military government. Between 1603 and 1868 (Edo period), the city Edo developed into one of the biggest cities in the world, with a population of over one million by 1700. Its name was changed to Tokyo (east capital) when it became the imperial capital in 1868.

The population of the main city is over 9 million people; with the closest suburbs the total population exceeds 13 millions. The world's most populous metropolitan area is Tokyo, with circa 35 million people, and it also is the world's largest urban agglomeration economy, with a GDP of $1.479 trillion at purchasing power parity. The city is home for 51 of the Fortune Global 500 companies, the highest number for any city. The tallest structure in Tokyo is Tokyo Skytree (a lattice tower, 634 m, 2012).

Oxford: On St Aldate's St, 200 m north of Broad Walk, 80 m east of Pembroke College, Tom Tower (1682, bell (Great Tom, rung 101 times (every 12 seconds, it takes 20 minutes) at 9 PM every night) tower) over Tom Gate, the main entrance to the majestic Christ Church College (1546, 431 undergraduates, 250 postgraduates, the second wealthiest Oxford college (after St John's), produced 13 British prime ministers), leads into its grand Tom Quad (inside).

- communications at the world level
- telecommunications
- networks
- peaceful nuclear energy use at the world level
- safety
- waste
- electrical power
- oceanic analysis at the world level
- atmospheric analysis at the global level
- meteorological service and prognosis at the global level
- world resources analysis
- sustainable use of world resources
- geographical and geological activity
- product safety at the global level
- hazardous material and chemical safety
- government broadcasting (radio, tv, Internet, newspaper, etc.) including news, scientific and technical information
- private broadcasting will continue, but the world government must be able to directly inform the people, without intermediaries
- space exploration and expansion at the world level – very important for the future
- patent and trademark
- intellectual rights
- all government work, which can be done by private companies, will be contracted with the best and reasonably priced private companies. At the same time, the government should always have competitive services for people – from plumbing and electrical help, to mortgage and buying or selling a house.

France, Paris: The marble statue Véturie ou Le Silance ou Vestale (1695) by Pierre Legros II (1666 – 1719), placed in 1722 on the east side of the Basin Octogonal in Jardin des Tuileries (created in 1564 as the garden of Palais des Tuileries (1564 – 1883, which was located between le Pavillion de Marsan, at the west end of the north part of Musée du Louvre, and Pavillon de Flore, at the west end of the south part of Musée du Louvre)).

# Proposition 6. Elections every 20 months

6.1. The Advisers should be elected every 20 months for one term only. If an Adviser X was elected for a term T1, then the next term T2 will have another Advisor Y. For the next term T3, X can be elected again, but the next term T4 will have a new Adviser, and so on. All levels of Advisers (minimum age 25 years) can be elected, not consecutively, at most 4 times (maximum 80 months = 6 years and 8 months).

6.2 All the employees in Government will respect Seneca's (circa 1,960 years ago) aphorism "To govern is to serve, not to rule", and Hippocrates' (over 2,400 years ago) aphorism "Make a habit of two things: to help; or at least to do no harm."

6.3 Advisers should have exceptional results obtained from their work, and based on these results, plus modesty, moderation, good character, friendliness, sharp mind, wisdom, good morals, and intense desire to help people, they will be elected, without any campaigning, publicity, fundraising, donations, debates, propaganda, political parties, advertising, or similar activities.

6.4 There will be use of advanced digital technology, which opens up entirely new opportunities for developing direct elections, and public control of the institutions, improving the transparency of the election procedure, and taking into account the interests and opinions of each voter (over the age of 21, who are not in a special medical institution for bad behavior or for mental health).

6.5. An Election Commission of 110 representatives from the 10 regions and from the 100 sub-regions, elected separately for 5 years, will have to examine the qualifications of all the candidates for Advisers, and for other senior management positions. Unqualified candidates will be asked to improve their qualifications, and then to try again later.

London: From the right bank of Thames looking southeast to the northwest entrance of Greenwich Pier, 10 Km southeast from Tower Bridge.

Greenwich, northeast side of the British tea clipper ship Cutty Sark (1869, out of service 1954, volume 2,725 m$^3$, weight (displacement) 2,100 t at 6.1 m depth (draught), length 85 m, beam (width) 11 m, sail 3,000 m$^2$, speed 32 km/h, capacity to transport 1,700 t, crew 30).

6.6. It is important to refresh the management, and to bring new people to help the big family of 7.7 B people. The older generations, who performed well, will be retained in important roles, because experience and maturity count very much. At least two months before the retirement, they will kindly be asked to transfer their expertise to the younger generation. Even after retirement, they will occasionally be invited to share their expertise.

6.7. In every election, with every winner, will be other two for number 2 and number 3. The number 2 and number 3 for each management position will be used when number 1 is not available (vacation, sick, etc.). They will constantly work for number 1, helping to solve urgent problems for the people.

6.8. Good elections are essential for the future.
There has been a tendency to make elections conflict generating events, with lots of propaganda, false information, heavy donations, unpolite confrontations, bully fundraising, hostile political parties and organizations, unlimited power ambitions, etc.

This will be completely changed into clean, friendly elections, in which people choose between leaders with outstanding results, plus talent to lead people to peace and freedom, modesty, moderation, good character, friendliness, sharp mind, wisdom, good morals, and intense desire to help people – no campaigning, no publicity, no fundraising, no donations, no debates, no propaganda, no political parties, no advertising, or similar activities.

6.9. All Advisors should also be local Administrators – they must show that they are good managers, and produce practical results for all people.

Oxford: On St Aldate's St, 140 m north of Tom Tower, the south side and entrance (right) of the Museum of Oxford (1975, in the former premises of the Oxford Public Library), a history museum of the City and University of Oxford, from prehistoric times onwards, with original artifacts, Roman pottery, details about King Charles I of England (1600-1649, king 1625-1649, who had Oxford as his stronghold), Oliver Cromwell (1599-1658), etc.

## Proposition 7. World Referendum

7.1 - An electronic world referendum will be organized every three months. The main questions will be:

1. Are you satisfied with the Government?
2. What Government work is good?
3. What Government work is not good?
4: Suggestions for improvement:

7.2 - Within two months after each referendum, the Government will respond to the people. Based on the suggestions received, new pro-people rules will be replacing some old rules.

Italy, Venice: Palazzo Flangini (right) and other palazzini on the north bank of Canal Grande, 220 m east of Ponte degli Scalzi.

## Proposition 8. Complete Disarmament

8.1 - Arms will not exist anymore, and only the police will have some small arms. Those who want arms for hunting or sport, will borrow them from police stations, with proper documents, rules and payments.

8.2 - All military units will become strong civilian organizations, working to improve the quality of life for everybody.

8.3 - For practical reasons, the transition from the current imperfect situation to the much better Sustainable Peace and Prosperity Structure (SPPS) will be very smooth: first - all the countries remain as they are, and they will begin – for example on January 1st, 2021 - to negotiate total and complete disarmament, with the help of the United Nations, for 3 months. Then for 5 months will intensely work to eliminate all the arms – either transform them in peaceful tools, or destroy them. Then a continuous verification and monitoring will be implemented, the make sure that the world finally achieved complete disarmament forever!

Oxford: On Merton Street an entrance to Corpus Christy College (1517, founder Richard Foxe, the Bishop of Winchester, 12th oldest college in Oxford (1st University College (1249, 2nd Balliol College (1263), 3rd Merton College (1264)), 249 undergraduates, 94 postgraduates), situated between Merton College (1264, founded by Walter de Merton (1205-1277), Lord Chancellor to Henry III (1207-1272) and later to Edward I (1239-1307), and Catholic Bishop of Rochester (1274-1277); Merton College Library (1373) is the oldest functioning library in the world), and Oriel College (1326).

## Proposition 9. Census every 5 years

A census will take place every 5 years – starting, for example, on October 1$^{st}$, 2023 - and all people will receive a special credit card (SCC), with their photo and other personal data. The delimitations between regions, and between sub-regions, will be adjusted by the census.

Japan, wind turbine working on the north-west part of the Inzai (Chiba) campus of Tokyo Denki University, 34 km north-east of Tokyo.

Oxford: From Merton Street, looking southeast to the north (left) and west (right) facades of Merton College Chapel (1294, 1425, 1451, the church of Merton College (1264, the third oldest in Oxford)); there were plans to extend this church to the west (right), but the land was leased in 1517 to Bishop Richard Foxe (1448-1528), who founded Corpus Christy College (1517), next door (west) to Merton.

## Proposition 10. Special Credit Card (SCC)

The special credit card (SCC) will be used to buy everything, to identify for voting, for census, for travel, for medical assistance, etc.

The current private credit cards will continue to work as usual.

The changes of the delimitations between regions, and also sub-regions, will be inputted on these cards, and no other work is needed.

Finland, Helsinki: a Baltic Sea canal from west to east, near Ruoholahdenpuisto, seen from a bridge on Bottenhavsgatan, near Helsinki Conservatory of Music (left).

Oxford: From Merton St. looking south to the northern façade of the main entrance of Merton College (1264). Important personalities associated with Merton College are British chemist Frederick Soddy (1877-1956, Nobel Prize in Chemistry (1921)), poet T. S. Elliot (1888 in St Louis, U. S. – 1965 in London, England, Nobel Prize in Literature (1948)), British philosopher John R. Lucas (born 1932), British mathematician Sir Andrew Wiles (born 1953, proved Fermat's (1607-1665) Last Theorem (1637) proved after 358 years).

## Proposition 11. People are something sacred for people

The enemies of the people on Earth are not other people, but viruses, microbes, bad bacteria and hundreds of deadly illnesses – all people on Earth will work together against these real enemies for all of us.

Italy, Venice: Palazzi Contarini (left), Gritti (center) and Vendramin Calergi (right), north bank, 340 m east of Ponte degli Scalzi.

Romania, Sibiu (Hermannstadt), 11 Oct 2008, from Strada Centumvirilor, looking northeast to the northwest side of Samuel von Blumenthal (1721-1803) National College (1380, center right, the oldest German-language school in Romania), and to the west part of the Lutheran Cathedral of Saint Mary (1520, 73.34 m high steeple, famous Gothic-style church).

## Proposition 12. Non-violence and medical assistance

12.1 - Non-violence is a strict requirement for all activities on Earth.

12.2 - The first rule for everybody on Earth comes from the Hippocratic Oath: Primum non nocere - first do not harm.

12.3 - Medical doctors and assistants will make regular home visits to all people, to keep them healthy, and to prevent illnesses.

Finland, Helsinki: in the south of the Railway Square is the Ateneum (1887, a major museum of classical art).

# Proposition 13. Truth only and collaboration

13.1 - People need only truth in order to create a long term peaceful and harmonious society.

13.2 - If someone lies – medical treatment will follow.

Japan, Mount Fuji (3,776 m, 1707 last eruption) seen from Kawaguchi city (left), near Kawaguchiko (Lake Kawaguchi, 6 km$^2$, 830 m elevation, right), 100 km south-west of Tokyo.

## Proposition 14. Freedom is required

14.1 - Freedom is a fundamental requirement on Earth.

14.2 - It is well understood that this freedom refers to doing good things in a civilized manner, not for war, violence or similar bad things, which are against the wellbeing of the people.

14.3 - Freedom goes hand in hand with responsibility.

14.4 - People can assemble peacefully only.

14.5 - For economy it is clear that the free market economy, while not perfect, gives the best results, but all people will have the option to choose between friendly private services, and friendly government services. Independent assistants and monitors will make sure that there are no abuses. Sine qua non requirements for happiness are morality and free market.

14.6 - The religion should be free, and is expected not to interfere with activities of the Advisors, and actually should help people.

14.7 - People of course can petition the small Word Government, and can change it anytime, if it does not perform as expected.

## Proposition 15. Spending less than revenue

All budgets will have surplus of 2% - there will be a strict application of the Latin aphorism: "Sumptus censum ne superset" (Let not your spending exceed your income).

Italy, Venice: Palazzi Belloni Battagia (right) and Ca' Tron (center-left) with Rio Ca' Tron between them, 370 m east of Ponte degli Scalzi.

# Proposition 16. Correcting errors

16.1 - Correcting errors is a permanent duty for everybody - Darwin (circa 140 years ago) said "To kill an error is as good a service as, and sometimes even better than, the establishing of a new truth or fact."

Japan, 13 km north-east from Mount Fuji, the easternmost and largest of the five lakes, Lake Yamanaka is also the third highest lake in Japan, standing at 980 meters above sea level.

## Proposition 17. Kindness is a necessity

Kindness is a requirement for everybody.

Seneca (circa 1,960 years ago) said "Wherever there is a human being, there is an opportunity for a kindness."

This is a fundamental idea which must be constantly applied.

USA, New York (1624): on Broadway, close to Times Square, and to Times Square Tower (2004, 221 m, 47 floors).

USA: Plymouth (1620, 60 km southeast of Boston), Plymouth Rock with year 1620 when the first ship Mayflower arrived in America.

USA: New York, from Brooklyn Heights looking northwest to Manhattan, with the two famous World Trade Towers (center, 1973-2001).

# Proposition 18. Government mobility

18.1 - All levels of government will be highly mobile - changing of the capitals for the 10 regions, and for the 100 sub-regions, etc.

18.2 - It is necessary to move the government close to the people, to be able to quickly solve the local problems.

18.3 - Locally the people will decide how to better organize themselves, to be more efficient and harmonious, with the help of the world government when necessary. Like in any big family, there will be differences in organization and management, based on their abilities and objectives, but all must be peaceful and harmonious. Conflicts will be promptly resolved by the medical personnel, police, and other assistants.

USA, Boston (founded in 1630): visiting tall ships from many countries, at the Boston Fish Pier (opened in 1915).

## Proposition 19. World Police and Assistance

19.1 - The United Nations will change in 2-3 years (for example, by 2024) into World Police and Assistance Organization (WPAO), to help local police in case of big natural disasters or big accidents, and will report to the top 10 Advisers. They will be located in all capitals, and help the locals. When an emergency appears, they will quickly move to solve the emergency.

19.2 - The police powers will be limited, and they will know and be friend with all the people in their jurisdiction – this is the key element of a civilized and peaceful Earth. If they notice a person with bad intentions, they immediately retain that person and call for a medical assistant (and other assistants, if necessary), to analyze and solve the issue very quickly.

19.3 - Police will be people's friends everywhere, and they will always help people.

19.4 - Prevention of bad events is the main objective of everybody. If a bad event occurs, the police and their assistants will eliminate the consequences, reestablish the normal situation, and determine why the bad event occurred, in order to improve their activity, and prevent such bad events in the future.

19.5 - Private property cannot be taken for public use, without just compensation, decided by at least 5 assistants.

19.6 - A person cannot be deprived by government of life, liberty, or property, without having several doctors and other assistants agree: for life – at least 12; for liberty – at least 6; for property – at least 3.

19.7 - A person cannot deprive another person of life, liberty, or property, which, unfortunately, occurs very frequently in the world, and very much effort and energy will be allocated to prevent such bad events.

France, Paris: The central part of the northern façade of the south side of the Cour Carrée du Louvre (1550), which is the oldest part, in the east side, of Palais du Louvre (1550), built around the Old Louvre (1150).  On the other side of the Champollion gate there is Jardin de l'Infante, then Pont des Arts (1802-1804, 155 m by 11m) and l'Institute de France (1795, grouping five Académies, including l'Académie française (1635) and l'Académie des sciences (1666)).

19.8 - In order to prevent bad things, the police, doctors and their assistants will be in permanent contact with all the people, by visiting them, phone calls, e-mails, tele-videos, and mail, to keep everybody calm and happy.

Italy, Venice: Palazzi Erizzo (left), Soranzo (center) and Emo (right), on the north bank, 400 m east of Ponte degli Scalzi.

USA, New York, the southwest side of the Chase Bank building
(1957-1961, 60 floors (plus 5 below ground), 248 m height, 213,675
m², 37 elevators) on Liberty Street, seen here from Pine Street
looking north (Nassau St after the building, William St to the right),
president then David Rockefeller (1915 (age 101 in 2016), studied
at Harvard (1936 cum laude), London School of Economics, and
University of Chicago (1940, Ph. D. in economics), worth $3.1 B).

## Proposition 20. Non-stop working

About 66% of the people of the world are working at any moment. Therefore, non-stop working of all world government departments – especially medical, police, emergency, volunteers – will be carefully organized.

Finland, Helsinki: The Three smiths statue (by Felix Nylund, 1932), with the Old Student House (1870, left) and Tallberg's house (right). On the base: MONUMENTUM – CURAVIT – LEGATUM – J. TALLBERGIANUM – PRO HELSINGFORS A.D. MCMXXXII ("The statue was erected with the help of a donation from J. Tallberg by Pro Helsingfors in the year 1932").

## Proposition 21. Privacy of discussions

21.1 - In order to have serious and constructive discussions and negotiations, they must be private.

21.2 - Privacy and discipline are necessary for good government work.

21.3 - The results will be public and preserved, but not the private discussions.

USA, Washington, DC (1790): the entrance to the Smithsonian Institution Building (1849-1855), on Jefferson Drive SW.

Australia, Sydney: 80 m southeast of Sydney Opera House, looking northwest to the southeast side of the Opera.

Australia: the entrance of the Sydney Harbour Bridge (1932, 134 m height (the tallest in the world), length 1,149 m, width 49 m).

# Proposition 22. Polite and harmonious government

22.1 - It is a strict requirement for the top management, and for all others, to be highly civilized, polite, courteous, harmonious and efficient.

22.2 - Who wants to work for the world government must have good manners.

22.3 - Harmony in the world starts from the harmony and good manners of the people in the world government.

Finland, Helsinki: a tall ship in the tourist harbor, in the south-east part of the city.

USA, New York, from Brooklyn Heights looking northwest to Manhattan, with the two famous World Trade Towers (center right, 1973-2001).

# Proposition 23. Transformation in friendship

23.1 - All conflicts must not only be quickly resolved, but they must be transformed in friendships. This is very important for long term stability.

23.2 - The medical personnel and others will work diligently to make sure that disputes are resolved, and then a friendship is developed. Only in this way the situation will become stable.

23.3 - People want peace, freedom, health, friendship and prosperity, therefore conflicts should be quickly resolved, and then the corrective medical treatment will include the transformation of hostility and aggressiveness into harmony and friendship.

Italy, Venice: Palazzo Buldu (center and right), on the north bank of Canal Grande, 500 m east of Ponte degli Scalzi.

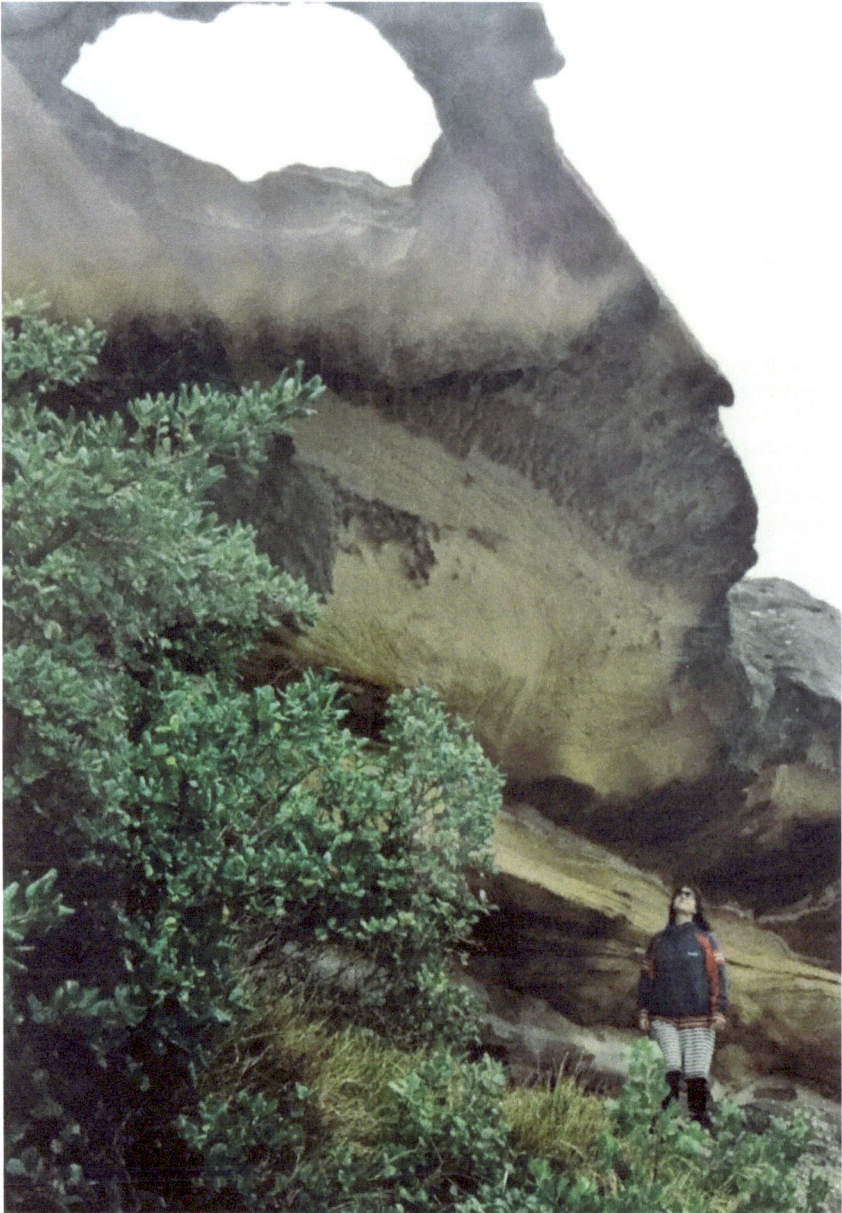

In eastern Australia, in south-eastern Sydney, 20 km south of the Sydney Opera House, 16 km southeast of the Sydney central business district, on the west shore of the Pacific Ocean, 80 m northeast of the Bare Island (discovered by James Cook in 1770), 200 m southwest of the Congwong Beach, 200 m southeast of Lapérouse Museum, looking up to a rock with a hole in the center.

## Proposition 24. Easy Communication

24.1 - As a single big, over 7.7 B, family on Earth, all people must be able to communicate easily with each other.

24.2 - For this reason, a common language and alphabet on Earth are needed. Because English is a de facto common language now, it will be taken as the basis of the world language, let's call it Mundo, which will be taught in all schools, and used in the world government. All the other languages will continue as secondary languages.

24.3 - The same is true for the Latin alphabet, which will be used everywhere, with other alphabets as secondary.

24.4 - The teachers will have a very significant role in implementing this proposition.

Rome, Vatican, Piazza San Pietro (1667, by Gian Lorenzo Bernini): Basilica di San Pietro (1506, center back), granite fountain by Carlo Maderno (1614, center, north side of piazza).

Sweden, Malmö, from Skeppsbron looking north to the north part of the west side of the Central Station (right), sign for Trelleborg and Limhamn (to left), Goteborg and Hamnen (straight).

France, Paris: L'Église de la Madeleine (or L'Église Sainte-Marie-Madeleine, or La Madeleine, 1842), a Roman Catholic Church in the 8th arrondissement of Paris, designed by Napoleon in 1806.

# Proposition 25. Global wealth for Peace only

25.1 - The 2018 Global Wealth Report from Credit Suisse shows that the total global wealth has reached $317 trillions (circa $41,000/person), which is encouraging, and all this wealth must be used only for peace.

25.2 - Like in any big family, there are differences, because some work more, some spend less, some move faster, and, especially, some are sick – this is the main reason for differences: not all people can be equally sick, some people are sicker than others. However, all the people and the government will work to help each other.

25.3 - It is a major responsibility of the Government to increase the global wealth, and to train those in need to have better working abilities and opportunities.

France, Paris: Jardin du Carrousel and Pavillion de Marsan, at the west end of the north part of Musée du Louvre; it also was located at the northern end of Palais des Tuileries (1564 – 1883 demolished).

Japan: The north side of the Osaka Castle (1597, 58 m, by Toyotomi Hideyoshi, rebuilt, with a museum), 5 km southeast of Shin-Osaka.

Japan, Osaka, ladies in kimono (means thing to wear, now it is very formal and polite clothing, generally worn with traditional footwear (zori or geta) and with split-toe socks (tabi)).

## Proposition 26. No bureaucracy

26.1 - No bureaucracy – this is required by all people, and every day attention will be given for improvements in this direction.

26.2 - In a well-organized country, with all people working together in harmony, this can be accomplished in several years.

Italy, Venice: Palazzo Fontana, with Rio di San Felice (left), on the north bank of the Canal Grande, 530 m east of Ponte degli Scalzi

Australia: Sydney: From the Royal Botanic Gardens looking to the southeast side of the harbourfront Sydney Opera House (1959-1973, right) and the Sydney Harbour Bridge (1932, left).

Australia: Sydney: A big tree in the Royal Botanic Gardens, south of the Sydney Opera House, with the Sydney Harbour (center left).

# Proposition 27. No corruption, no duplication

27.1 - Everybody will work really hard to completely eliminate corruption, organized crime and drug trafficking.

27.2 - Constant attention will be focused on avoiding duplication at all levels of the world government – there must be continuous collaboration between all levels, to prevent duplication, and to eliminate it, if it was found.

USA, New York (1624): on Broadway, between 50th and 51st Streets.

Slovenia, Ljubljana: 2 Nov 2009, statue of France Preseren (1800-1849, educated at the University of Vienna, the greatest Slovene poet), at Cyril and Methodius Square (80 km northeast of Trieste).

USA, Boston: 3 Dec 2009, from Avenue Louis Pasteur (1822-1895, French microbiologist), Boston Public Latin School (1635, Schola Latina Bostoniensis, the oldest and first public exam school in US).

## Proposition 28. World reserve system

28.1 - Each government department will have some reserves for special situations (natural disasters, big accidents), and the banks will also have good financial reserves.

28.2 - All people will be encouraged to save some money in banks with 5% interest.

Finland, Helsinki: the Railway Square, east of the railway station, with the Finnish National Theatre (1872 - 1902).

Australia: the North Cronulla beach (300 m, highly hazardous, being unprotected on the Pacific Ocean) looking south to the Cronulla city.

Australia: The Three Sisters sandstone rock formation (center left, on the south edge of Katoomba (1879, 8,000 people, elevation 1017 m, 110 km west of Sydney, 39 km southeast of Lithgow)).

## Proposition 29. Integrity and efficiency

29.1 - Inspectors will help the Government with the integrity and efficiency issues – always there are ways to improve the work.

29.2 - Inspectors will give advice regarding integrity and efficiency, and will take corrective actions when necessary.

Italy, Venice: Palazzo Sagredo (right), on the north bank of the Canal Grande, 580 m east of Ponte degli Scalzi.

Romania, Brasov (Kronstadt), 12 Oct 2008, looking northeast to the Town Hall, with Piata Tricolorului and Bulevardul Eroilor (down).

Japan, Kawaguchiko, 22 Nov 2008, looking south to the north façade of Kawaguchiko Station (on the Fujikyu Kawaguchiko Line, terminal station, moving only to the left (southeast)) and the northern side of Mount Fuji (3,776 m, 1707 last eruption).

## Proposition 30. Family assistance

Because all families need assistance from time to time, and the big 7.7 B family on Earth contains billions of small families, all of them will have the assistance they need – this will be the result of one country well organized and managed.

Finland, Helsinki Central railway station (1907 – 1914), on Brunnsgatan, in the city center

Australia: From Manly Beach (10 km northeast of Sydney Opera), looking to the west of Pacific Ocean (165,250,000 $km^2$, 46% of the Earth's water, 33% of all surface area, larger than all of the Earth's land, 10,911 m the deepest point in the world at Mariana Trench).

USA, California, from Pacifica State Beach (south of San Francisco), looking to the east part of the Pacific Ocean.

## Proposition 31. Living in harmony

Because all people on Earth want to live in harmony right now, it will be relatively easy to implement this in one good and civilized country. This may include having small, beautiful and commonly agreed fences around properties, because good fences make good neighbors, and also helps with more privacy.

USA, New York (1624): on $42^{nd}$ street, close to $8^{th}$ Avenue, inside a tall building, three sculptures of people waiting at a door.

## Proposition 32. Dispute resolution

32.1 - Dispute resolution is not only Government's obligation, but it will be everybody's duty.

32.2 - There will be professional assistance from medical personnel, police, people assistance specialists, volunteers, religious organizations, and many others, but the bottom line is that everybody must avoid disputes.

32.3 - When there are different opinions, just stay calm, express your opinion, listen to others, and continue calm the discussion until a compromise is reached.

32.4 – There is no need to spend much time and energy – let the people decide, and even if your idea is not temporarily accepted, there are chances that in the future you'll have more people agree with you.

Rome, Vatican, Basilica di San Pietro (1506): the sculpture in Carrara marble Pietà (1498–1499, moved to the first chapel on the right around 1750) by Michelangelo Buonarroti (1475 – 1564). It is the only piece Michelangelo ever signed.

Japan, Kyoto, 25 Nov 2008, 100 m northwest from Kyoto Station, 30 m south of Shiokoji Dori, looking northeast to Kyoto Tower (1963, 131 m).

## Proposition 33. No abuses

33.1 - Special attention will be given by Advisors to avoid abuses and wrong interpretations of the rules. All assistants (doctors, mathematicians, CEOs, engineers and teachers) will closely monitor all activities, to avoid abuses and wrong interpretations of the rules.

33.2 - This requirement of not having abuses is demanding – but this is a general job, not only for Government, but for everybody, as part of the big family, we just don't need abuses.

33.3 - The abuse, in some places, of confiscating the land by some government bureaucrats will be eliminated – the land belongs to the people, not the government.

33.4 - The abuse, in some places, of having trains, airplanes, and others making unhealthy noises, with the government support, will be eliminated – peoples' health has always priority.

33.5 – The abuse, in some places, of having to change the clocks twice a year will be eliminated – only the normal local time zones will be used.

33.6 - If abuses are observed, they will be immediately reported to the Government, and corrected, in general, by the People Assistance Department, which will have personnel, including medical assistants, to analyze and promptly solve the abuses.

Italy, Venice: Palazzi Michiel di Colonne (left) and Mangilli (center-right), north bank, 630 m east of Ponte degli Scalzi

Australia, Sydney Monorail (1988, closed after 25 years in 2013, 3.6 km, connected Darling Harbour (in photo), Chinatown and the Sydney central business and shopping districts, 8 stations, 6 trains).

## Proposition 34. Free commerce

34.1 - In one country, with one market, the commerce between the people on Earth will be free of taxes, tariffs, duties, etc. – plenty of opportunities for everybody.

34.2 - The speech will be free and responsible. It is expected not to call for war, violence, or similar destructive activities. People want peace, freedom, health, friendship and prosperity.

34.3 - The press will be free and responsible. It is expected not to call for war, violence, or similar destructive activities. People want peace, freedom, health, friendship and prosperity.

34.4 - People can assemble peacefully only, with police for help. It is expected not to call for war, violence, or similar destructive activities. People want peace, freedom, health, friendship and prosperity.

Paris: Tour Eiffel (1889, 324 m, looking north-west); a boat moving downriver on la Seine, Port Debilly (up, near pont d'Iéna).

Japan, Tokyo Metropolitan Government Building, 243 m, 48 floors,
1991, in Shinjuku, with two observation decks on floor 45, 202 m.

## Proposition 35. Jobs for all

35.1 - There will always be plenty of jobs at world minimum wage (assisting other people, for example), and the standard situation will be this: more jobs than available people, so people will choose the jobs they like the most.

35.2 - No unemployment, no homelessness, no begging – just all working harmoniously, having good houses, and helping each other.

London: The northwest façade of the Old Vic Theatre (1818, 1871, 1902, 1927, 1938, 1950, 1960, 1963, 1985, 2003, 1067 capacity), on the corner of The Cut and Waterloo Rd., a traditional playhouse with big name actors (Laurence Olivier (1907-1989)) and top directors.

## Proposition 36. Limited number of rules

36.1 - All rules proposed by Advisers must be approved by their 5 assistants (doctors, mathematicians, CEOs, engineers and teachers), and for any new rule over 2,000 basic rules (each rule on at most half a page, total 1,000 pages), at least on old rule must be eliminated.

36.2 - All the rules can be changed or eliminated when a majority of the people or their Advisors agree, but some fundamental peace and order rules will remain.

UK, London: From the Shard (244 m), looking northwest to the southeast side of St Paul's Cathedral (1675, 1697, 1711, 158 x 75 x 111 m).

## Proposition 37. Constitution improvements

This Constitution of the World can be improved when 66% of the voters agree.

Italy, Venice, Palazzo Ca' D'Oro, north bank, 580 m east of Ponte degli Scalzi.

## Proposition 38. General ideas

38.1 - The purpose for all people on Earth is to be healthy, to live in peace, freedom and harmony, to be prosperous, and to prepare to expand to the Moon, asteroids, Mars, and other places in the Universe, which can support life.

38.2 - Important immediate objectives for everybody are:
- Reserve time for happiness.
- Use robots and automated processes, work less, and spend more time with your family.
- The weekend will be like a small vacation.
- Prevent burnout.
- Make civilized behavior and harmony everywhere an important issue.
- Eliminate stress.
- Help friends and colleagues.
- Keep everybody relaxed, calm, friendly, patient, and happy.

38.3 - To start this new structure of the world, one idea could be this: the first Honorific World Observer (from UN, for example) could invite 10 Presidents form big countries (like USA, China, Russia, UK, India, France, Japan, Germany, Brasil, and Egypt) to be the first 10 Advisors Level 4, starting, for example, on January 1$^{st}$, 2021, for 10 months, until November 1$^{st}$, 2021, when the new calm and noiseless elections will take place. The same for the 100 Advisers Level 3, and so on.

38.4 - For better understanding and easier implementation of this Constitution, the following books, by Michael M. Dediu, are recommended:
- Our Future is Sustainable Peace and Prosperity – Moving from conflicts to harmony and peace
– Our Future Depends on Good World Educations – Moving from frail education to solid education.

Japan: In Shinjuku, from the 45th fl., 202 m, of Tokyo Met. Gov Bg South Tower: Shinjuku Mitsui Building (224 m, 55 floors, 1974, left), Shinjuku Center Building (223 m, 54 floors, 1979, center), Mode Gakuen Cocoon Tower (204 m, 50 floors, 2008, right up), : Keio Plaza Hotel (180 m, 47 fl, 1971, right).

– Friendly, Helpful & Smart World Management - Moving from bureaucracy to responsive world management
– If You Want Peace, Prepare for Peace! – Moving from preparation for war to preparation for peace
– World with One Country & its Ten Friendly Regions - Moving from 195 disagreeing countries, to 1 country with 10 collaborating regions
– After 10,000 Years of Conflicts, People want 10,000 Years of Harmony - Moving from continuous wars to stable peace

Finland, Helsinki: the Railway Square, east of the railway station, the bus station (left) and the Finnish National Theatre (center-left).

## Proposition 39. Extensions

This Constitution of the World is valid not only on Earth, but also on the space around Earth, on the Moon, Mars, asteroids and any other places were the very good people on Earth will be moving in the future.

Italy, Venice: Palazzo Rava (center), on Fondamenta del Vin Castello, south bank, 250 m south of Ponte Rialto.

# Proposition 40. Intentions and putting into practice

40-1 - This Constitution of the World is intended for at least 10,000 years of harmonious living on the happy Earth.

40.2 – The present Constitution of the World is ready to come into force, and to be put into practice, for the benefit of all people on Earth, on 6 March 2020, and it is ready to remain into force, and enjoyed by all people at least until 6 March 12020.

UK, London: From the Shard (244 m), looking north to 30 St Mary Axe (center right conic, 2003, 180 m), the Leadenhall Building (2013, 225 m, center back with XX), the Heron Tower, the Lloyd's building, etc.

Japan: In Shinjuku, from the 45th fl., 202 m, of Tokyo Met. Gov Bg North Tower): Shinjuku Sumitomo Bldg (210 m, 52 fl, 1974, center), Shinjuku Mitsui Building (224 m, 55 floors, 1974, right).

# Auspicium Melioris Aevi (Hope of a better age)

Italy, Venice: The south end of La Piazzetta, the south part of Piazza San Marco, with gondole, and a wedding picture of a Japanese couple.

www.ingramcontent.com/pod-product-compliance
Lightning Source LLC
Chambersburg PA
CBHW041310210326
41599CB00003B/52